light

by Jessa Rose Sexton

light

Copyright 2022 by Jessa Rose Sexton
ISBN 978-1-7342711-9-5

Written by Jessa Rose Sexton
Book Block Design by Whitnee Clinard
Edited by Rosemary J. Hilliard and Jordan Russ
Hand Lettering by Ara Vito
Cover Art *Leaves the 99* by Rebecca Hunter

All rights reserved. No part of this publication may be reproduced or transmitted in any form or by any means without written permission of the author.

Cover art used by permission of the artist.

Special thanks to Rehanna Mae Grant, Jordan Russ, and Ara Vito for their feedback and encouragement.

Published by
Hilliard Press
a division of
The Hilliard Institute for Educational Wellness

Franklin, Tennessee
Oxford, England
Abbeyleix, Ireland
www.hilliardinstitute.com

light

by Jessa Rose Sexton

*I want to shine a
your darkness*

LIGHT *so bright on you*
RUNS *away.*

Why Me?

Who am I that I should go? That I should

be called to step into this fray, to stand

in this moment when I know others would

be better, brighter, bolder than I can

ever even imagine to be. Why

me? I'm too weary, too weak—and I get

(far too often) in my own way. When I

speak, I'm too awkward or too arrogant—

or some dangerous combination of

the two. Why. Me. There is an entire

world *full* to choose from. Yet I feel your love,

your favor, on *me*. Somehow you are sure

of me, even—and especially—when

I am not. Lead me anyway. Amen.

Waymaker

When the world tells me *there is no way*, I
know The Waymaker. And I don't say this
lightly or as one who's never asked "why"
or pleaded into the dark emptiness
of my own heart, "Lord, I believe. (I do.)
Help my unbelief," but as one who *must*
say it, because I've seen it. Seen Light through
nothingness, shining a way ahead. Just
ahead. And it wasn't always the way
I wanted—the way I'd planned. And I didn't always want to walk it—I won't say
otherwise to seem holy—yet, amid
that weary walking . . . I knew He was there.
No matter my wandering—He is here.

Psalm 63

You, God, are my God. And I'm looking for you. Honestly. Actively. I'm empty without you—lost in a dry land, thirsty in the endlessness of my own wandering, of my own wondering. And I'm *sure* of your presence. I have *seen* your glory . . . yet still I seek—still I find my story veering into the desert. And still your greatness, your goodness, and your justice remain. My God, your love is better than life itself—and because of this: I. Must. Sing. I must praise. I must pursue. I must rejoice always because—even when I might stray—I'm seen by you, my God and my King.

Zephaniah 3:16-20

Gather me up in your arms—oh Lord—I

know full well that you are present and yet—

can I admit (*should* I admit?) . . . and why

do I ask when there's nothing here you'll get

as new information anyway—still

I ask you: How do I move into the

quietness promised by your love? When will

I hear the radiance of your loud sing-

ing? I feel like it's time already—time

for my oppressors to be dealt with, for

all the fortunes they depleted—once mine—

to be finally and fully restored.

I'm just saying—these hands *are* growing weak.

Your promises hold hope. When will they speak?

Psalm 146

Praise the Lord, my soul. Every single day. As long as I live. No one else in authority—no one else *at all*—can save me. In a temporal world, you, Lord, abide. And that's why I can't help but sing: because ultimately, my trust isn't with the weak or fleeting. No. I trust the Creator of the heavens and earth; the faithful Caretaker of anyone in need—the freedom-giving, clarity-bringing, ever-faithful, ever-present, indeed *only* sure sustainer and confirmed King. And so, with Hope full and Vision restored, my life reflects the refrain: "Praise the Lord!"

The Least of These

Okay, just to be clear: when we talk a-
bout those who need the Grace of God, I'm on
the front line, often unable in the
moment to ignore past mistakes I've drawn
all over this life. However—knowing
that *cannot* and *should* not keep me from wor-
ship, from telling you about Him, showing
you His love—although I feel so unwor-
thy for the task. But that thought, you see—that
feeling is just the enemy telling
me what he has learned will keep me from *at
least* seeing the Light and *at most* being
the Light. No. I *refuse* to let him win,
though I might fight this battle quite often.

Isaiah 40

Do you not know? Do you not understand?
The Lord is our everlasting God (Who
was and is and is to come, through and through
and through), the Creator of all earth: land
and sea and you. Even when life is demand-
ing or difficult—He will give to you
the strength that you need in your weakness to
make it through. You are weary, yes, but stand
in the promise of His presence. And know
this: you don't have to be enough. I re-
peat: *you don't have to be enough*. No one
is, on her own. But you aren't alone. Go
ahead and stretch your wings without worry.
He is here. You will fly. And you will run.

YOU are weary, yes, but stand in the promise of HIS presence.

Isaiah 61

The Spirit of the Sovereign Lord is here with me—not because of me or anything I've done, but because of you. You need to know good things are on the way, to hear comfort is coming. You are free from fear of others—and of the captivity of your own brokenness. You are released from the ruiners of your past. Despair cannot hold you back from the mighty ways He will grow you for His glory. Nothing will hold Him back from this promise—or dim this everlasting joy: our Lord is faithful, He is here, and goodness is coming. Let everyone and everything Praise Him.

Follow You?

You say, "Follow me," but I'm not ready.

There's so much to do in preparation—

so much baggage from my past weighing me

down and holding me back, and I'm not one

to jump into something all willy-nill-

y. I've got so much to do before I

can be of any real value. I will

get there—but I'm not there yet. Look: here's my

lengthy list of everything I need to

work on and work through to become even

slightly effective or useful to you—

I'm utterly unqualified till then.

You know this—but you still ask me to go.

I'm not ready. But I still will follow.

Shadrach and Co.

I don't have to answer to you. My God is bigger than your idols. My God is faithful, and worthy of faithfulness. Rod and staff at the ready, He will bring His comfort to me in any and all circumstances. Including now. His mighty love and providence are the same yesterday, today, and tomorrow. He can bring deliverance to me in any and all circumstances. Including now. Yet, even if He doesn't, I'd rather stand in the fire with Him than in counterfeit causes with you. And through this, you'll see how He is always with me. Including now.

Despair CANNOT hold the mighty ways for HIS

HE will grow you back from glory.

Fix My Eyes

Dear God—I don't really understand how I can feel so heavy and so light at the same time. Though I suppose that's life down here. The world is heavy. Christ is Light. That brings some comfort. But—I'm just going to be honest about this: I'm. Still. Hurting. I'm still reeling right now in this all-too-real juxtaposition—and today's being overtly overwhelming from my soles to my soul. And yet. And. Yet. Dear God—I don't stop feeling your presence. And I see, even in the darkest darkness a sometimes-only-speck shining always. And . . . let me fix my eyes there always. Amen.

Even Me

Lord, let no one stand in the way of my fulfilling the purpose you have for me—no plot to divert your goodness or pry me from your path. No selfish motives bringing my attention elsewhere. Oh my God, let no darkness blot out your Light shining through me. No loud, ignorant voices prodding me away from you, encouraging me to my ambitions. Oh my God. It's me. I'm the one in my own way. I'm the one with endless distractions, endless lists of excuse after excuse without a single real reason. And yet I still stay. Oh my God—get me out of my own way.

Oh my God, let no darkness blot out your LIGHT shining through me.

Why? When...

I want to be open and honest with

you, God. (As if you don't already know

what I'm thinking or feeling now—as if

you aren't big or holy enough to hold

me through my anger or my fear or my

joy even—as if pretending I'm not

where I am right now for the sake of . . . Why?!

Why *do* I ignore the fact that I've got

a struggle with my struggle? That I can't

pull myself out of a pit by contin-

uing to cover myself with dirt, plant-

ing myself not in your goodness but in

a suffering I'm afraid to bring to

you—why? When everything in me needs you.)

The Lord Is Near

"The Lord is near." Right. Now. And that's the comfort I carry side by side with my grief. That's the last strand left at times, keeping some certainty in my heart that—though beneath me is a fall I couldn't withstand—I. Will. Not. Fall. I'm still hanging on. To You. And You are near. Right now when I can't find any silver lining inside the truest emptiness I have ever known—all I know is *You are near*. All I know is You are near. As I lie here, my soul sprawled, raw with wondering why. As night changes into night with no sign of sun, I've found a light in this: "the Lord is near." Right. Now.

As night changes
with no sign of
light in this:
Right.

into night
sun, I've found
"the LORD is near."
NOW.

April 5, 2020

God being the same yesterday, today, and forever has a slightly different meaning to it now—with every day feeling vaguely like the last as weeks blur into the next. I've never felt so much consistency and inconsistency all at the same time. What I mean is—such a lack of normality has now become the new norm. And some days that's easier to deal with than others. Some moments easier to breathe through than others. We all have lost something to this pandemic's stay. Yet, we remember: There. Is. Hope. In the feelings and fears, always: There. Is. Him.

Because You Are Holy

Lord, you are holy. And because of that I come to your throne boldly and I pray for strength right now. I know you can heal what has been wronged or broken. That you can stay this ache. Lord, you are holy. And because of that I bring you my hope. Not a loose impractical dream (I mean, what good does that do anyway?) but faith-founding truth. You are a God who hears me, knows me, sees me, and listens to my heart even when it can't speak. Lord, you are holy. And because of that (and my life) I know you've been here all along. Be here still. Perform an all-out miracle as only you can.

Tapestry

I was thinking the other day about

how my testimony isn't really

one moment. It's one thread woven throughout

the entirety of my life. The weav-

ing is more dense in spots, looped over and

over into a rich illustration

of His nearness and my fullness in Him,

like a scene by Cézanne. Other times one

single faith thread, barely visible a-

mong the darkness surrounding it (but, squint

and stand close—you will see it), is all the

image offers—but still. It's there. Present

always. So it's not a testimony,

per se. More like a working tapestry.

Consuming Power

Holy Spirit—gift and guide, dwelling in me, making me a temple, a vessel, a voice. For Him. Melting away the dullness and pain of my past, for only then can I stand in His brilliance. Only then can I stand. Before Him I lay low, full only of my own emptiness and pulled only by my own dreams. Where I have been is not where I am. Praise. The. Lord. For I have been in darkness—and now I see His Light. The God of Hope has somehow seen fit to overwhelm in me hope, joy, peace—by the consuming power of the Spirit.

Romans 15:13, 1 Corinthians 3:16

I Still

Stuck—but not stagnant. Down—but not defeated. Exhausted—but not empty. Today I am trying to sort through these complete complexities that are now everyday life. But they're heavy. And make sense only half the time. I tell myself that it's okay—to mourn lost and delayed dreams, to be appreciative for the side of slowing down that has made me more aware of what matters, to seem light one moment and weighed down the next, to feel both lone and loved. It's okay I don't really understand because through it I know this: even here, when I can't perceive, I still persevere.

You are a God who and listens to my heart

HEARS me, KNOWS me, SEES me,
even when it can't speak.

Advent: Day 3

Son of God you are: a promise fulfilled

from a long line of waiting. Born humbly—

you were our greatest gift. Baptized holy—

you were our utmost example. You thrilled

your Father and astounded the crowds. See—

no one expected *you* to be *you*. Yet

you, as you, were perfect: everything we

never deserved, never can earn—a debt

of infinite proportions repaid in

love by Love. And I cannot understand

(no matter how many sonnets I build)

why you would go from On High to lowly;

how you can be All as you can only.

Son of God you are: a promise fulfilled.

Advent: Day 10

We waited thousands of years for a Savior: the first promise fulfilled to come between what came between. Sin removed us, gave us a reason to strive when before we simply thrived, disconnected us from our Creator and put us at odds with His creation, took away any ignorance of death. And the only trade for this—for the lives of many—was the life of One. The Son of God—Emmanuel—who came humbly and lived humbly, who showed love and was Love, who (though sinless) came here to live for our goodness and die for our sins. So we can stand again in God's presence.

Advent: Day 22

He who is mighty has done great things for me. Holy is His name. His mercy is lavish and ready for those who adore, admire, and live in utter awe of His greatness. He has shown His strengths again and again—to me, to others, to the whole world, seeing through our thoughts and understanding our very hearts. He lifts the humble, fills the empty, serves the servant—even when we walk away from Him. And it's all because of this overarching theme: in everything—everything—He. Is. Faithful. And I want my whole life to reflect: He who is mighty has done great things for me.

On the Third Day

On the third day, you separated the

land from the waters, bringing green and growth—

fruit and flowers of all kinds. Later, clothed

in these leaves, Adam and Eve were sepa-

rated from you. On the third day, in a

plague of complete darkness, the great Pharaoh

refused to see Light, bringing more sorrow

to his people before your people es-

caped. For three long days Esther fasted, Jo-

nah suffered, Saul was blind. And your parents

searched for you. Through it all, the world made way

in waiting for Emmanuel to go

before us. Instead of us. We're saved since

you died and lived for us. On the third day.

Psalm 91

Live in the shelter of the Most High. Rest

well in the shadow of the Almighty.

Because, listen—I don't know everything,

but I know this: He alone is my re-

fuge. He alone is my ultimate es-

cape. When the world threatens, He is safety.

I can trust Him. Always. In everything.

He will cover me in His faithfulness

like feathers. He will protect me under

His wings—and He will do the same for you.

Just believe. Just wear this truth like armor

against your foes—and your fears. Don't wonder

how you'll go it alone—He'll see you through.

He'll walk it with you. Now and forever.

Who I'm Called to Be

Maybe my goal should be a little less self-confidence (because, honestly, my record's fairly flaw-filled, so that's a recipe for disaster (right?) . . . and yet I keep coming back to this like it will somehow be different *this time* (right?)). Maybe, just maybe, I should veer my focus, come around to a new perspective of seeing that *true confidence* comes when I'm living *as* and growing *in* who God has called me to be. What a determinative, personally earth-shaking shift! What all could I create for Him? What tenacious impact bring—if I embraced my purpose.

Where I have BEEN is not where I AM.
Praise. The. LORD.

Anxious for Nothing

"Be anxious for nothing." But how the heck

do I do that? Like, practically . . . in real

life in this sometimes (honestly) straight wreck

of a world when sometimes (honestly) I'll

blame the world when really—really—the truth

is: It's. Me. I'm the one dousing this flame

in the fuel of my continual, ruth-

less need for approval (I know it's lame;

I'm trying to be vulnerable here.),

proclivity toward comparison, and

quirk of getting in my head, staying there

for way too long for my own good, expand-

ing on reason after reason I must

not be enough. No wonder I'm anxious.

Imago Dei

I am made *imago dei*—in the image of God. But what does that mean? Because, I'll be honest: often when I look in the mirror, I don't see Him; when I pause to think through my *many* mistakes, I don't see Him. Yet, there are no conditions linked to how I am made. But how do I own it? And live it? Well, what are His distinct qualities? The Word says (again and again) that He is Love. He is Light. So being made in His image means I am a reflection, a refraction, of who He is. And that makes this a profound part of my purpose: to shine the light of His love.

1 John 4:8, 1 John 4:16, 1 John 1:5

Grief: A Pantoum

Grief hits us all

at different times,

different

ways.

At different times

because of the varied

ways

we all process,

because of the varied

people we are.

We all process,

though. Eventually.

People, we are

different—

though, eventually,

grief hits us all.

Love, Love, Love

The repair of the world:

the Living God has been actively

working this mission,

and I have been asked to join Him—

to go therefore into the world

(not of the world)

to love

and be loved

by Love

      for Love.

Daniel 3

Even if He doesn't—

He can.

Even if He doesn't—

He is.

A Daily Prayer

Equip me.

Expand me.

And step in to fill all the spaces

where I am not enough.

Amen.

A Second Daily Prayer

Get behind me, Satan.

Go before me, Father.

Walk beside me, Jesus.

Shine within me, Spirit.

Amen.

Despair CANNOT hold the mighty ways

you back from HE will grow you for HIS glory.

I'm

looking up.

And it's like the sun

wants to shine,

but it doesn't know how to burst

or even peek through the clouds.

Some days

are like that.

But I keep

looking

up.

I am utterly flawed

and blessed

to be loved

by you.

Only a moment ago

the Sun was hidden

behind that cloud,

and you were in darkness.

But now—

Its brilliance

covers you.

What a difference

a moment makes.

I want to shine a light

so bright

on you

your darkness

runs

away.

*You are a
KNOWS me,
to my
can't*

God who HEARS me, SEES me, and listens heart even when it speak.

Nothing new under the sun—

    Except me.

    Except you.

    Except His mercies every morning.

I want to be

your shield,

your sword,

your parachute.

Your weighted blanket.

Your weightless escape.

But all I can be

is here.

I cried out to the heavens,

"God, where are you?"

And He answered

not from the skies

but by my side.

I am a poem.

    Carefully crafted

        to speak your name

        in every line.

Thankful for your grace

        in my mistakes.

Sometimes struggling

        (yet always striving)

        for rhythm and rhyme,

        for passion and purpose.

Unfinished—

I cried out to the heavens,
"God, where are you?"
And HE answered
not from the skies
but BY MY SIDE.

One Week of Devotionals

DAY
1

Read

Why Me?

Who am I that I should go? That I should be called to step into this fray, to stand in this moment when I know others would be better, brighter, bolder than I can ever even imagine to be. Why me? I'm too weary, too weak—and I get (far too often) in my own way. When I speak, I'm too awkward or too arrogant— or some dangerous combination of the two. Why. Me. There is an entire world full to choose from. Yet I feel your love, your favor, on me. Somehow you are sure of me, even—and especially—when I am not. Lead me anyway. Amen.

Reflect

When the Lord told Moses to be the one to bring His people out of captivity, Moses questioned His choice. Moses questioned His process. Moses questioned his own ability. Why me? The same question I ask today. Later in Hebrews 11, Moses is listed among the "heroes of faith" as we often call them. I'll admit I find a little comfort knowing he ends up there when he starts with *why me?*

And can I be honest? The ending of this sonnet was a struggle. Because I want to offer myself up (Lead me anyway.) because I believe His confidence in and love for me means something. But sometimes it takes a while to utter those words. If sonnets didn't have to have such a strict structure, I'd probably put a line break, or twelve, before the submission. But, as it is, please know you aren't alone if it takes you a while to go from *why me?* to *lead me.* Even Moses gave a lot of excuses, needed a lot of signs, and ended up with a helper for the journey given to him.

You aren't alone. And He is sure, even when we are not.

Answer these questions, in your heart or on the paper:

1. How have you felt inadequate to answer His call?

2. Who else in the Bible is a perfect example of an inadequate person who did wonders for the Kingdom?

3. Read the poem again as a prayer, or use your own words to pray God will lead you even in your uncertainty. And know He is sure of you, always.

DAY

2

READ

Waymaker

When the world tells me *there is no way*, I know The Waymaker. And I don't say this lightly or as one who's never asked "why" or pleaded into the dark emptiness of my own heart, "Lord, I believe. (I do.) Help my unbelief," but as one who *must* say it, because I've seen it. Seen Light through nothingness, shining a way ahead. Just ahead. And it wasn't always the way I wanted—the way I'd planned. And I didn't always want to walk it—I won't say otherwise to seem holy—yet, amid that weary walking . . . I knew He was there. No matter my wandering—He is here.

Reflect

Again and again I write on the theme of God's presence. Through all. And, actually, this sonnet is basically collection of consistent themes in my poetry: a favorite verse (Mark 9:24), my word of 2021 ("light"), a rebellion against what the "world" tells me, the previously mentioned steadfastness of His being here, and my rawness in admitting I don't have it altogether.

I don't always understand His ways. I often stumble along the way. And I struggle with frustration when things don't go my way. But I have a hope that becomes a light to my soul, even in the moments that feel like nothing is left, that feel like emptiness. I pray for this light in your life. Today. Tomorrow. And always.

Answer these questions, in your heart or on the paper:

1. Is there a theme, a consistent message you see God weaving throughout your life?

2. What "way" is before you that seems impossible or impractical to walk?

3. Read the poem again as a prayer, replacing "He was, He is" with "You were, You are." Or use your own words to acknowledge that God can make a way—and ask Him to do so for you.

DAY
3

READ

Psalm 63

You, God, are my God. And I'm looking for you. Honestly. Actively. I'm empty without you—lost in a dry land, thirsty in the endlessness of my own wandering, of my own wondering. And I'm *sure* of your presence. I have *seen* your glory . . . yet still I seek—still I find my story veering into the desert. And still your greatness, your goodness, and your justice remain. My God, your love is better than life itself—and because of this: I. Must. Sing. I must praise. I must pursue. I must rejoice always because—even when I might stray—I'm seen by you, my God and my King.

Reflect

Until today, I'd never noticed how David, in Psalm 63, is praising God so mightily . . . from the desert. He's in a place where he says he's "earnestly seeking" God, so he feels some sort of distance from Him, and *yet* he still praises and *yet* he still sings. And *yet* he still knows the power—and the love—of his God. Even in the desert.

And it makes me think about my deserts—the ones I get myself into because of my own stupidity or selfishness as well as the ones I find myself in because sometimes the world and certain people in it are straight crap. But in all those cases, His presence has remained. And so I should sing. Even in the desert.

ANSWER THESE QUESTIONS,
IN YOUR HEART OR ON THE PAPER:

1. What is a time you've been in the desert? Are you in a desert now?

2. How have you seen Him in that time? How do you see Him now? If you feel like you don't see Him, He's here. Talk to Him.

3. Read the poem again as a prayer, or use your own words to tell Him of your struggles, loneliness, or pain—and admit (to yourself?) that He is here. If you don't feel it right now, keep drawing near to Him. Keep. Drawing. Near.

DAY

4

READ

Zephaniah 3:16-20

Gather me up in your arms—oh Lord—I

know full well that you are present and yet—

can I admit (*should* I admit?) . . . and why

do I ask when there's nothing here you'll get

as new information anyway—still

I ask you: How do I move into the

quietness promised by your love? When will

I hear the radiance of your loud sing-

ing? I feel like it's time already—time

for my oppressors to be dealt with, for

all the fortunes they depleted—once mine—

to be finally and fully restored.

I'm just saying—these hands *are* growing weak.

Your promises hold hope. When will they speak?

Reflect

Too many times we hold back from praying what we're thinking . . . as if God doesn't know anyway. In this instance, I think about how we will (okay, I'll speak for myself only here)—how I will read His promises and think, "Yes, I believe this will happen. But. When?" Or I read about a coming restoration, and I think, "Yes, I believe this will happen. But. When?"

I don't admit to understanding God's calendar. And I know I'm supposed to bring everything to Him in prayer "with thanksgiving" as Philippians 4:6 says. But sometimes I just want to ask Him to hold me, hear me, and heal me.

I *know* radiance is coming. But some days it feels further away than others. This chapter in Zephaniah feels that too. Through it all—"I know full well you are present."

Answer these questions,
in your heart or on the paper:

1. Are there any promises you're holding to right now that you're waiting anxiously to be fulfilled?

2. Are these true promises from Him, or things the world has told you that you deserve? What's the danger in confusing the two?

3. Read the poem again as a prayer, or use your own words to tell Him—honestly—the desires of your heart: whether they seem superficial or deep, just talk to Him. Ask Him to sort out where you should be striving, and what you can let go of so you can start thriving.

DAY

5

READ

Psalm 146

Praise the Lord, my soul. Every single day. As long as I live. No one else in authority—no one else *at all*—can save me. In a temporal world, you, Lord, abide. And that's why I can't help but sing—because ultimately, my trust isn't with the weak or fleeting. No. I trust the Creator of the heavens and earth; the faithful Caretaker of anyone in need— the freedom-giving, clarity-bringing, ever-faithful, ever-present, indeed *only* sure sustainer and confirmed King. And so, with Hope full and Vision restored, my life reflects the refrain: "Praise the Lord!"

Reflect

The Lord deserves my praise. There is no one and no thing like him. Only He will remain and sustain. Only He will bring salvation and completion.

This is comfort. This is inspiration to praise Him always. And, just like Fanny Crosby's lyrics ring out, "This is my story. This is my song. Praising my savior all the day long." Because He is Lord—I can't help but sing. And in that singing, my life points others to Him.

Answer these questions, in your heart or on the paper:

1. What is your preferred way to praise the Lord—to worship? Singing? Reading the Word? Serving others?

2. Find ways to work worship into your days, consistently, for the next 30 days. Make a plan. Follow the plan. Add in the ways of worship that come naturally to you, and other ways as well.

3. Read the poem again as a prayer, or use your own words to praise Him!

DAY

6

READ

The Least of These

Okay, just to be clear: when we talk about those who need the Grace of God, I'm on the front line, often unable in the moment to ignore past mistakes I've drawn all over this life. However—knowing that *cannot* and *should* not keep me from worship, from telling you about Him, showing you His love—although I feel so unworthy for the task. But that thought, you see—that feeling is just the enemy telling me what he has learned will keep me from *at least* seeing the Light and *at most* being the Light. No. I *refuse* to let him win, though I might fight this battle quite often.

Reflect

The enemy has a (nearly) perfect plan to keep me from living out Matthew 28:16 and John 13:34. He gets me so wrapped up in how completely flawed I am that I believe I'm not right for the job. That I'll be seen as a hypocrite because I'm flawed. That I'll be slow of speech and slow of tongue. How can I tell others about Christ if I'm not Christlike enough . . . if my words might be misinterpreted? Won't my damaged image damage His image?

Even sharing these poems is hard for me. Because these are the honest words from my heart, but what if they're misinterpreted as arrogance or my life doesn't line up to someone's vision of a poet who writes about the scripture and her Savior?

See—isn't it a (nearly) perfect plan? I spend so much time talking about how I'm not good enough that I forget He's more than good enough. I forget other people need to hear just how more than good enough He is. I stop looking upward and loving outward. I stop opening up.

The (nearly) perfect plan has one major flaw.

Don't be afraid. I'm right here. I'm your God. I'll strengthen you, help you, and uphold you with my righteous right hand. (Isaiah 41:10 paraphrased)

We don't have to be good enough. He's more than good enough. And He wants us to tell others that truth.

Answer these questions, in your heart or on the paper:

1. What is something that holds you back from sharing God's love to others?

2. What is something that holds you back from deep worship and connection to Him?

3. Read the poem again as a prayer, or use your own words to tell Him honestly what is in your way, and ask for a closeness to Him and a boldness to share His love.

DAY
7

Read

Because You Are Holy

Lord, you are holy. And because of that I come to your throne boldly and I pray for strength right now. I know you can heal what has been wronged or broken. That you can stay this ache. Lord, you are holy. And because of that I bring you my hope. Not a loose impractical dream (I mean, what good does that do anyway?) but faith-founding truth. You are a God who hears me, knows me, sees me, and listens to my heart even when it can't speak. Lord, you are holy. And because of that (and my life) I know you've been here all along. Be here still. Perform an all-out miracle as only you can.

Reflect

I have a few recurring prayers that are heavy in my heart. Either they seem too huge to hope for or they've been sitting around for so many years. I wrote the words in this poem with a faith that He is the *only one* powerful enough, holy enough, to answer the deepest desires of my heart.

But I need you to know something raw and true. When I read this poem, sometimes it feels like a deep declaration. Other times it's a weak whisper, with a hint of Mark 9:24 ("I believe, help me with my unbelief.") in my heart.

Sometimes I just need to pray these words because I need to hear myself say them.

It doesn't make you a hypocrite to be honest with the Lord. He knows anyway. Be bold in asking Him to answer your prayers and to brace your faith.

Answer these questions, in your heart or on the paper:

1. What's something you want to boldly ask of Him?

2. Why aren't you? Or, if you are, have you felt any of Mark 9:24 as you've prayed?

3. Read the poem again as a prayer, or use your own words to ask boldly The Holy One for the miracle you desire and the strength to hope in Him always.

4. If that prayer feels too hard right now, try this one:

Fix My Eyes

Dear God—I don't really understand how

I can feel so heavy and so light at

the same time. Though I suppose that's life down

here. The world is heavy. Christ is Light. That

brings some comfort. But—I'm just going to

be honest about this: I'm. Still. Hurting.

I'm still reeling right now in this all-too-

real juxtaposition—and today's be-

ing overtly overwhelming from my

soles to my soul. And yet. And. Yet. Dear God—

I don't stop feeling your presence. And I

see, even in the darkest darkness a

sometimes-only-speck shining always. And . . .

let me fix my eyes there always. Amen.

I WANT TO BE
your shield,
your sword,
your parachute.

your weighted blanket.
your weightless escape.

BUT ALL I CAN BE
is here.

About the Poet

I remember the first time I wrote something someone else said was good. And I thought, *Huh, I bet I could make a career out of this.* And then I wrote seamlessly for the rest of my life.

Okay, that last part is way off. Writing is an ebb and flow. But it's my love. And I've been at it professionally for over a decade now. That includes my time in the world of publishing and editing (14 years there), in education as a professor of literature and writing (11 years there), as well as my current career as a senior editorial writer.

Oh, and then there's the poetry. There's always the poetry. I'm constantly scrawling out a poem. And then another. And then another.

This book is a compilation of some of those scrawlings.

www.ingramcontent.com/pod-product-compliance
Lightning Source LLC
Chambersburg PA
CBHW051653040426
42446CB00009B/1119